A PLEASURE TREE

A
Pleasure
Tree

Robley Wilson

UNIVERSITY OF PITTSBURGH PRESS

Published by the University of Pittsburgh Press, Pittsburgh, Pa. 15260
Copyright © 1990, Robley Wilson
All rights reserved
Baker & Taylor International, London
Manufactured in the United States of America

Library of Congress Cataloging-in-Publication Data

Wilson, Robley.
   A pleasure tree / Robley Wilson, Jr.
     p.   cm. — (Pitt poetry series)
   ISBN 0-8229-3635-6. — ISBN 0-8229-5427-3 (pbk.)
   I. Title. II. Series.
PS3573.I4665P57   1990
811'.54—dc20   89-39345
                                        CIP

Some of the poems in this collection first appeared, often under different titles or in slightly different form, in the following magazines:

The Atlantic ("A Pleasure Tree"); *Bits* ("Pets"); *Black Warrior Review* ("The Man with the Blind Wife"); *Carleton Miscellany* ("The Parting" and "Trans-migrations"); *The Colorado Quarterly* ("Say Girls in Shoe Ads: 'I go for a man who's tall!' "); *Colorado State Review* ("The Mechanical Cow"); *Commonweal* ("My Son, Drawing a Picture"); *The Georgia Review* ("Shadows"); *The Hudson Review* ("Yankee Poet"); *The Iowa Review* ("A Pastoral for Institutions"); *The Malahat Review* ("Against Violence"); *Midwest Poetry Review* ("Thinking of the Moon," "the BIRD pursues the BEE and KISSES it," and "Byzantium Again"); *The New Republic* ("The Sniper in the Tower" and "Lines for Later Anniversaries"); *Ontario Review* ("And You Think"); *Open Places* ("Renting," "Love/Love/Love," and "Bridesmaid"); *Plainsong* ("I Wish in the City of Your Heart"); *Poetry* ("In Early Morning Traffic," "The Mornings I Oversleep," "Keys," "What You See," and "Company Cafeteria"); *Poetry Northwest* ("The Diver," "The Lovers," "Defoliation," and "When We Are Old"); *Tennessee Poetry Journal* ("A Fear of Crowds"); *Three Sheets* ("The Parable of the Cat"); *The Virginia Quarterly Review* ("A Valediction," "Giraffe," and "Blake's Tyger, Wilson's Cat").

"After Love" was first published in *I Love You All Day / It Is That Simple* (Abbey Press); "Leaving the Body" and "Fame" first appeared in *Returning to the Body* (Juniper Press).

*The publication of this book is supported by grants
from the National Endowment for the Arts
in Washington, D.C., a Federal agency,
and the Pennsylvania Council on the Arts.*

Contents

Contents

A PLEASURE TREE

The Diver

At the tip of the high board,
looking down, I am not yet
concerned for the green water,
not yet ready for plummeting
hands-first in fathoms of air,
and if someone notices me as
she squints against the light
rippling the flags of towels,
I am too remote to take her
into account. I stand, loose,
musing the length of my body
so any looker-on might think
from this posture I am a man
praying. Appearance fools us.
I am involved in myself, see
the foreshortening of a man
whose sweat jewels his chest,
whose trunks are a blue belt
holding body and its potency
in a respectable compact; my
thickened legs, as resilient
as the board they rise from,
sway my weight like birches.

I inch forward, trembling in
the shimmer of sky, a bird
nervy on his perch the moment
before he flies; set my toes
over the brink of the board,
curling them down as if they
alone were all the grip a man
should need on risky actions.
I can make out around the pool
the figures and colors summer
draws among the idle. I know
every girl at her naked ease,

3

every miracle of smooth line
young bodies carry; I follow
the otter-heads above water
and the funhouse legs beneath.
From such a height I can tell,
as from a cloud, the praises
I owe everything except soul,
and when, an instant from now,
I bow my whole self-possession
outward and earthward, spirit
will turn me to angel over all.

The board under my movement
commences music, my muscles
beat countertune and my sweat
springs in the body's corners.
Rhythm: tattoo of the blood
to the cushions of my feet;
behind me on its steel hinge
the thin board rocks me awake.
Plank-walker, pirate-of-air,
I throw my two fists forward,
thrust out from the tall tower
just as it topples over. Un-
clenching the hot sky, I hurl
it over my head. One moment
I am a man swimming the void;
the next I am diver, graceful
in his precipitous element.
I wear the agile wind, I see
faces and bared white throats
craned toward me. I dazzle
across the eyes of the girls;
my hands carve ahead of me
only their perfect turbulence.

What You See

We were talking again about
auras—you see them, you said,
white only, never in colors—
and how with your eyes looking
through me, looking at a point
around which I am perhaps
whirling—gathering myself,
my nervous energies, as stars
pull themselves together to die
terribly against the universe—
looking into me, astrological
darling, and having found out
my center, my null, my heart,
you make my aura manifest.

It too is white, you say.
A flicker of light dispels it,
a confusion of background
breaks it into dark slivers
you cannot reassemble, a flag
in your attention turns me
back into the mere body I was.
For now, I am hanging on
by a psychic ribbon secured to
the pushpins of your eyes—
my soul is a high-wire dancer
supposing itself weightless,
but what you see is the linen
parasol I spin for its balance.

Renting

The walls need pictures, the floors
carpeting, the windows narrow curtains
to catch whatever August sunlight
comes here untainted by green maples.

The lady who lives downstairs thinks
I am married, and knowing what wives
know sees nothing barren in these rooms
but dwells instead on her utilities:

She waits for my wonder at the bath,
the kitchen with appliances included,
dependable heat and water, closets
ample, two keys to a private entrance.

I ask to be left alone. I sit down
in the middle of the largest room
and hold my eyes closed until I hear
her calling her cats to the back door.

Safe. I imagine you living with me
in this cheap apartment. The floors
are of varnished boards that shine
from within and require no carpets;

the windows are like whitened frames
where I see you standing, looking out
as if you are amazed how the world
is like green glass and the sky gold,

and when I turn my gaze to the walls
they are transformed into a gallery
displaying all of your absent selves.
I am determined to keep this place;

I will say to you, *It is miraculous:
We have a secret way in, every room
glows, there is even a deep alcove
for stealth, for dancing in bare feet.*

A Valediction

This is a picture of the car we owned
More than three years ago; I miss it—
The one we have now burns oil and gets
Fewer miles to the gallon than the ads.
Here you are, relaxed, leaning against
The fender; see how the paint glistens
In that afternoon's sun, and a nebula
Of light glares from the hood; look at
The lustre of chrome and curved glass.
Nothing was ever wrong with that car—
There was not a scratch on the finish
Or, except for the dog, the upholstery.

On this slicked paper you are wearing
The brown skirt with the funny buttons,
And the plain white blouse. Your feet,
Not in the picture, are surely bare.
It had been a humid, electrical month,
So your hair, sensitive as all of you,
Is straight and uncared for; it never
Held claim on beauty, or voguishness.
You're smiling. Had I said something?
The natural world seems oddly tropic—
An overhang of limbs and long leaves,
Fuzzy evocations of an empty jungle.

Yet it is only the square, dead world
Of the Midwest—the flat land clipped
From magazines and stuck in the album
Your Eastern school friends made for you
As a joke. How sybilline they were—

To argue for life, to think this paper
Copies reality, is to invent too much
From shadows. This is a fake, found out
In desk cleaning. There is no more car,
No more tropics, and no more ardent boy
Aiming a camera to document a stranger.
It is Sunday; children are in the house.

Love/Love/Love

When you coaxed me to believe
one "ought not foreclose any
possible alternatives,"
I laid aside the prospects
for burrowing in your love
like the worm into satin
and became a common moth.
Not that I find it pleasant;
I spiral about the rooms
of fashionable virgin
ladies who turn up velvet
kisses for me to brush at,
but seldom have I glided to
the point. They taste of you:
my Phantom of the Boudoir,
you dress my mannequin loves.
Out-of-date clothes in the mind's
deep closets—luscious buried
mistress! Now I have forgot
in what style we used to serve
for each other's appetites,
and being no moth for flame
I grow starved enough to light
on any threadbare lover.

In Early Morning Traffic

She has risen early, bathed, made up the bed;
she has put on in the warm, curtained room
yesterday's clothes; she has had coffee and toast.

Looking out the bright window above the sink
she has memorized wind, the gold clouds, the one
blue junco unsteady on a hawthorn branch.

It is the last day of winter. Walking to the car
she lifts one hand to catch the blown hair away
from her face. She looks back: the junco is gone.

Then she is into traffic—anonymous, private again.
You see her this morning, one hand high on the wheel
balancing the first cigarette, her eyes troubled

with daylight and the letting hold of dreams,
her mouth in the small shape of worry. She drives
in the dull motorcades: to work, or the airport

out of town, or the day's busyness—or to a home
that cannot run for long without the competence
she has practiced to master. She drives;

the seat belt is drawn against her body
like the weight of a lover. It is no use
following while she remembers someone else.

Company Cafeteria

Left to ourselves, we chat about betrayal.
We agree to its usualness, she wonders
out loud if love ever happens without it,
I shrug and rest my elbows on the table;
she knows my mind too well to talk about it.
We share our lunch, agree to meet on Monday—
Remember, she says, *I owe you an apple.*

My Son, Drawing a Picture

Snails, roses, and the ram's-horn crown
Aladdin wore—they are all the same
To him: things rolled tight as the tape
Which in God's infancy sized Creation.
The vanishing-line hypnotist's spinner
Measures his experience, and the fire
That celebrates July burns pinwheels on
His slow visions. He knows about mazes,
He assumes magic; a secret beginning
Unscrolls from the tip of his pencil.
Whatever makes a world—if nebulae
We cannot see like a screw's point
Augur through the heavens, or if
Blind lights like a babble of brasses
Uncoil infinitely while we are deaf;
If indeed eternity is as simple as
The braid rug wound under his elbows
And the tempered hearts of our clocks
Truly mediate the Icarian universe—
His mind compasses it easy and whole.
There will be no quarreling between
The snail he draws and the rose I see.

The Mornings I Oversleep

Nobody knows what is hidden
under this ocean; something
perhaps too ugly to be told.

All I care is: I am lying
on a yellow beach in summer
and the indigo tide is in,

floating the sun on its back;
gulls planing on the lucid sky
blow small sobs for kisses.

I am not occupied with depths,
as who is in this warm place?
Probably there are creatures

whose skeletons would reveal
the structure of times past,
cold-blooded occurrences, slime

cast in the image of nightmare;
I make no room for them here.
I shade my eyes so I may follow

the sly passing of beach girls.
I lean my elbows on the blanket
and the sweat on my back sizzles.

Leaving the Body

"When I wake up in the morning I have first to figure
out what language I was dreaming in."—Max Ernst

Now we begin to stir inside
the dream—like the birds
at the windows, whose lids
cover the black stones
of their eyes. I smother
my face against you, blind
in your soft hair, mute
at your throat, trying not
to wake. . . . Now, dreadful,
it is morning in the dream
as in the world; the light
eats out our eyes; the birds
are the shadows of wings
and the warm wind tells us
what it wants us to know.

After Love

After love, we can feel our caving in:
Muscle at the drawn corners of our mouths
Slackened, our eyes sinking under a swirl
Of gold lamplight, blue threads letting the lids
Slide closed. Our arms and legs like beams let go
Everything; we are debris so recent
The falling is still thunder in our heads
And the ground under it trembles and sways.

We go down—like two houses in a slum,
A neighborhood never to be salvaged
From its civilized corruptions—sometimes
From fire, sometimes from hired demolition,
Sometimes from rot, but always together
So no inspector sifting through our dust
Can tell one house from the other, or learn
How from each wreckage we rebuild ourselves.

Between the Men and the Women

1

It is the moment
matters, we tell you.
It is this moment.

It is like the flame
patient in dead wood
to take its freedom

and be ruinous.
It blackens the skies.
It leads to nothing.

Once it has taken
the life of a star
we are only blind.

Once in our frail bones
it does not let us
pretend we can dance.

2.

In the quaint ruins
age makes, the corpses
have no genitals.

They lie with faces
harrowing the ground;
their nails are broken.

Here is a woman
sent mad in her bed,
hugging her dead love.

Here is a woman
whose body is grain
nourishing no one.

Here is air and earth
in the great round O
of the woman's womb.

The Parting

I imagine traces of your skin
Caught under my fingernails like
An orange's veined secret flesh,
And for hours afterward I bear
The sharp odor of your sweetness;
My several senses stay married
To the memory of learning how
Your whole round virtue separates
Into its discrete perfect parts.
Lady measured by longitudes
Only, your body is grained fruit
Broken from the stems of my hands.

The Lovers

She is under him
like a rabbit
under a cat; quiet,
she seems broken,
and yet he is tense—
a machine wound
too tight to perform,
frightened of her.

Look here, closer:
a pulse visible
in her throat tips
you. Playing dead.
Figure what strength
she is reaching to,
like the rabbit,
like any hurt prey.

Her limbs glisten;
in her furred corners
droplets of light
melt against him.
See how her muscles
draw to their shortest
spans, how her teeth
show white and wet.

Now. Watch these two.
The cat has half-lost
his purchase; he is
astride unreason; he
lays back his ears,

freezes his hackles
to the shape of anger,
contains her thrashing.

At last he is a sure
predator. What is she
but a victim? and who
knows what she enjoys?
She lies under him
like a weak rabbit
under a cat. *Voyeur!*
Has he killed her yet?

Bridesmaid

Stripping the green tissue from the flowers
she is excited, and as she hugs the long stems
before the mirror in the bride's mad-house
she feels herself a flower—a pale, calm rose
undiscovered, beginning slowly to find shape.

In the glass as neutral as real air she sways;
it is a wind whose origin no man has learned
that bends her and teases her formal gown;
it is a light entering through shut windows
that colors her. No madness touches her.

At the ritual, by the slow procession leading
to the heart some say is God's, by the flutter
of words whose wings like hummingbirds' brush
promises from the moist lips of the lovers—
she is nourished, she bows, she is a garden.

Joining after joining she is the same beauty
fading in the same shadow. This is a formal
enclosure where the gardeners come and go
until she loses count; it is a solemn room
where the windows never break for loneliness.

The kisses of women sustain her. Her hands
waving goodbye become accustomed to the air
as if it were water. The riotous dresses
fill her closets and wait to be used again,
shouldering one another to be taken first.

Dogs

A woman I used to know
divorced her husband,
kissed her kids goodbye
and moved to Salt Lake
where she studied painting
and lived alone. Every
once in a while I'd get
a letter from her, chatty,
full of fond friendship,
How much I'm enjoying
new life. Then for a time
I heard nothing at all,
and I thought: That means
she's found someone else,
neither husband nor chum,
to share her visions with.

Then one day came a note;
she'd been on the fringes
of the city, her paints
and easel in the redwood
case she always carried,
when she was set upon by
dogs. *Insane but true—*
a pack of dogs gone wild
in a place you'd imagine
civilized, led by a German
shepherd cross—seven or
eight of them, she thought.
They knocked her down, tore
the flesh of her left arm,
bit the back of one shoulder
down to the bone. People
heard her screams; they came
running, stood and watched.

At last the police arrived,
chased off the pack, caught
two of them and carted them
off to the pound for tests.
I'm still in the hospital,
she wrote, *I have nightmares
you wouldn't believe. When
they finish the skin grafts
and the physical therapy
I'm moving to another place,
not Utah. The police wanted
to shoot the pair of dogs;
a citizens' committee got
an injunction to save them.
I've tried painting a little
but my muscles are sore and
the brush remarkably heavy.*

All of that comes to mind
when I hear others talk
about Salt Lake City, Utah:
thwarted love, the pleasure
of solitude, those wild dogs
kind people cared about.

Notes for a Vigil

*Something . . . someone's hand
being always at her lips,
blowing airy kisses across
ever-widening distances. . . .*
One ought not to attend
to the voices of the poets;
a confusion of sentiments
chokes us and it's possible
that our last words—words
wives and children, perhaps
even a lover or two, wait
around our deathbed to take
as the last gift of Age—
that our last words will be
someone else's. *Something
about someone's hand being
always at her lips, bidding
adieu. God, I don't know:
the poor man was delirious,
and anyway you never expect
sense out of men like him.*

A Pleasure Tree

In the tree that bears gold
apples, the starlings keep
drunken balance. Seven apples
remain, spared by windstorms
that have savaged orchards
down to bare limbs and torn
fields into windrows. A marvel:
Seven apples have not fallen,
but hang in these March rains
like brown jewels, inside them
the pulp turning to raw wine
amber and ruby and cold as air.

And You Think

If she abandons me
I will persist alone
in the mists that gown
the hollows at dawn,
will prop the orchard limbs
and share the apples
the wind drops—the best
for myself, the rest
a gift for the horses—
in the empty afternoons
will sit with books
under the cottonwood
in the near meadow
rustling, will take walks
to the ridge at sunset
in stiff alfalfa waiting
for the last cutting,
will sleep each night
like a dead man in a box.
All winter long
I will be a bare tree
dreaming blossom and fruit.
All winter long
I will lie under the snow
like the blind mole
with his patient heart.
All winter long
I will be a wire fence
bleeding rust.

Thinking of the Moon

We are excited, thinking of the moon,
as who would not be
to think of you, temptress, huntress,
pale and stalking us
through the February trees,
our eyes squinting tears
to drown the branches—as who
would not be tense with expectancies,
unreasonable mythologies, disquiet
that comes at dark in the short months—
and our damp breaths clouds
like a ring of weather circling you?

In the short months,
in the counting of our breaths,
in the measuring of all the words
that passed between us,
thinking of the moon and you,
the half-dressed mistress
filling our white nights,
we lay less claim to you
than to the skies—a discretion
between invention and love;
we exchange our calculations,
we write, we think, we are excited.

What happens when the moon is full?
What when she wastes?
At dark, in the shortest month,
we watch your failing and your flowing,

we are drawn to you and set back;
we are an indiscriminate ocean
seething, we fear being forgotten.
If to be excited is not to be in love,
then we have lost you,
stormy forever in our cold February—
like men in a fit
and a constant danger to ourselves.

The Parable of the Cat

"Three hours after taking the drug, the patient told of seeing a cat stripped of its skin; he said the cat was alive, and mewed at him piteously."—*a clinician's notes*

The parable of the cat
is the labor of the mind
as an instrumentation,
a mechanism with access
to infinite materials,
owing nothing to craftsmen,
nothing to the masters
and teachers who hire out
what they study from books,
nothing, nothing whatever
to the maker whose work
is Nature's most cunning.

In the cat are implicit
all our nameable desires,
conceits, self-seekings,
arrogances portentous
as God, final as murder;
all our accidental graces,
indiscriminate hungers,
our random affections:
all our darling vanity,
horror of every filth
except our own, the need
to be fondly mistrusted.

Further implied in the cat
is the sensuality we hug
up against our bellies,
the curious dilations
in our eyes when we face
love or death or violence,

the thickening of taste
(clotting of the saliva)
from no other stimulus
than a roused imagination:
in short, any chemistry
which releases the body.

The physiology of the cat
is an elegant striation
like rushes woven; pools
in hollows, rippled, slick;
color in whose intensities
the eye's estimable value
is opal and clear; threads,
as if the carcass bulged
out of such onion sacks
as old ladies shop with;
a perpetual slow current
eroding fleshy banksides.

The meaning of *this* cat
is ambiguous. Before us
on a porcelain surface
the beast lies, skin peeled,
limbs staked with chrome
pins, its blood sounding
like a persistent faucet
in a far room of the mind.
It is a toy of science,
and haunts us—a dream
whose continual miracle
is that we all share in it.

We are told that the cat
survives to this day
in a glass case lighted
and piped with oxygen,
still perfectly capable
of the natural functions,
a sweating of rainbows
whose perverse glitter
neurologists take down.
The man did not survive
who had this vision first—
nor is he, exactly, dead.

Giraffe

Because his heart
Is huge, and blood
Is pressed to reach
His altitude,

This complication
In his health
Preoccupies
Him with himself,

And though he owns
More heart than us,
It has not made
Him generous.

He is restrained
From doing good
By those machineries
Of the blood

Whose complex works
Show on his skin:
Reticulate
Outside and in.

A net dilates
Beneath his brain
To shutter tight
His jugular vein,

Lest, as he drinks,
The blood decline
By gravity
And drown his mind.

Thus when a thirst
Absorbs his thought
He need not fret
About his heart,

While in the dry
Blue airs above
He is too far
Remote for love.

Defoliation

No wind, say the trees,
Nothing for breath,
No natural decay
Ripe above ground,
But under—enough.

No leaves, say the trees,
No growing back,
Nothing green for your eyes,
No cool place,
No shade to lie in.

No seed, say the trees,
None of sowing
Nor anything to tend,
Nothing for rain,
No season to harvest.

Twenty years, say the trees,
Given or taken;
Nothing ends shallow,
But far down where
We meet and join.

No matter, say the trees,
The difference between
White root, white bone.
None care, say the trees,
Whose hurt, whose fall.

A Pastoral for Institutions

The pleasures of being mad
are common knowledge; right off
the top of your head, you

could name fifteen or twenty:
the high sense of yourself
is one—every madman his own

Voodoo doll, every lunatic
his own gleeful inquisitor.
Or the utter deep privacy

of the shuttered mind—that's
two—where the only visitor
is the devil possessing you.

Or the world's attentiveness
—clinicians, barbers, wives—
that's three through seven,

though the numbers matter
less than you might have thought,
and the order not at all.

The Sniper in the Tower

In my mind is a tree,
With time reaching its tap
To my blood's origins.
It thrives: its limbs fatten,
They crotch and crotch again,
Red leaves burgeon on them.

Checked by the bone-roof sky
The branches hug themselves;
The tree's crown is perfect
On the brain's armatures;
The foliage breathes out
An expense of oxygen.

The fruit is difficult:
A flower, solemn ripening.
A husk white as the moon.
My branches bend aside
To make a place for it;
Nothing in Nature is sterile.

At last arrives a season
When the portentous fruit
Breaks from the mothering limbs.
I lean with a mortal wind;
Far down on the black lawns
I watch my red leaves splashing.

Against Violence

In the dark night, in the vacant lots,
mothers are burying their babies—
you hear the scraping of the shovels
& the rough dirt tumbling in the graves.

It is humane, it is a recourse
the mothers choose in confronting war,
it softens the terror of the years
they must otherwise look ahead to.

The babies neither whimper nor cry—
you would not believe they are hungry,
or cold, or human. In the black fields
between the tottering tenements

the shovels turn & turn, the mothers
spell each other, the older sisters,
whispering, watch. At the opened windows
the fathers drink & strum the guitar.

Keys

Nothing suggests a man's power quite
as keys do. You notice, in public
buildings, in hallways and elevators,
men in blue shirts and dark trousers
who carry at the hip a chain heavy
with keys. You think: they might be
police, might be guards whose concern
is security—though where you expect
pistols in black holsters you see
keys, bunched on a silver-colored ring
like coarse jewelry, like broken metal,
like thin brass fingers, like a weapon
with difficult moving parts. Nothing
suggests a man's power quite like keys.

Imagine one morning a woman has forgot
the key to the office where she works;
imagine her frantic; imagine her knowing
she must get inside before her employer
comes to begin the importance of his day;
imagine her, helpless outside the door
while the man in blue comes toward her,
fumbling at his belt after the right key,
saying in his patient, fatherly voice:

Don't worry. It's all right. Trust me.
I can let you in to wherever you want.

Pets

For most, loving is being led.
They come to us as instruments
Whose life is function—are abused
When they are not handled, wasted
Unless they feel our management.

Others for freedom's sake resent
Touching—yet they are no less ours.
You know how cats come to your face
When you are half-awake in bed,
Breathe your breath, and are content.

Blake's Tyger, Wilson's Cat

The first blow hardly stuns my prey—
Flesh and feather that come my way;
Clod-wings too slow to think to fly,
They flop absurdly under me.

I let them loose only to judge
My spanning of the mortal bridge,
As if each bird pinned by my paw
Fulfilled old promises of law.

Do brown birds look before they die,
They see the tiger in my eye;
Sparrow-god witness to my kill,
Was ever life more ritual?

Even full-bellied, I protract
The pure aesthetic of this act
Into an art that dignifies
Creatures ignoble otherwise.

The Mechanical Cow

Marvelous four-cylindered beast:
switch on her tail and she muses
butterfat, clanking a brass bell;
between her armored quarters oil
gathers and runs to the shed floor—
watch your step. Every spring and fall
the co-op man dismantles her,
checks points and brushes, changes plugs
and sets her timing; once a month
the man from the commission stops
to analyze her milk—as if
anything could go wrong with *that*.
She ruminates on low-test gas,
combustion chambers so designed
as to be practically silent
in operation; she will run
night after night flat out, and is
(if there are children) tamper-proof.
Early mornings the farmer comes
into her stall, sets down his pails,
and strikes white sparks from her dugs.

Amnesty

Friend in Sweden,
I live in your house,
sleep in your bed,
look off damp mornings
through a dream of fog
to the real islands
we used to sail for.
At low tide the ledges
reveal themselves
and draw down gulls;
at the tide's height
sand sharks feed
on mackerel schools.
Nothing changes here
but proprietorship.
In this deep channel
is plenty of ocean
to quench all wars,
and time enough
to rescue us both
with the families
who sailed beside us.

Fame

Truly we want nothing else
and say—explaining it—
it is like our late friend
the watchmaker, a soldier
in one of the former wars,
who lost his leg just at
the knee to clumsy metal;
he said he could feel pain
in his toes, that he could
bear the pain but could not
endure the rage of being
helpless to touch the pain.

As for ourselves, all wars
are reportage hard to trust;
we credit our own lives
and think from time to time
of our dead soldier-friend.
Today in his peaceful town
we sometimes come inside
at dark from clearing snow,
wondering lazily
how long will pass before
the illusion we still wear
boots has left our legs.

Transmigrations

I imagine a long
death, my love, and a long dream
no one shares with me.
When I awake at last
this is the old familiar Nature
around me—the aisles through
the orchard littered
with small apples,
the golden shadows humid and
smelling sweetly of decay—
while off to the East
seen narrowly between the black
misshapen tree trunks
the summer meadow is on fire,
and skyward
in the best direction
sunlight whispers the edges
of black leaves and
black fruit and black limbs.
This is the familiar Nature,
but enormous, as in
the disproportions of a bad life.
At nightfall, rummaging
under the cold moon, my first
sense of your shadow comes
like a shaking-out of muslin
over the bed
I have hollowed in the meadow.
You are an owl; you are hunting
me. You plummet
out of the black wind over
my hiding place; your eyes
are like yellow shackles;

your broad wings drape the moon.
I cry to you: *Once*
we were lovers here! My voice
is a poor thin squeak,
my running is a rustle weaker
than the leaves make
blowing. I dance
hysterical circles under the grass
thinking: *What a trick*
death has done me, until
your talons draw my blood
and we begin to fly
together
into the endless dream.

2.

And if you were a cat,
I would need
to be a bird facing
those green eyes dilated on
God knows what chemicals having
to do with hunger; I
would need to be an object in
that mouth of yours with its
inscrutable lines
and its muscular shudder,
the flutter that bares the teeth,
the dry pink threat
saying: I will swallow you
whole,
I will swallow
you, I will
swallow
every freedom your wings

45

are too slow to rise to,
I will swallow your very life
and use it for
strength
to catch and kill your brothers—
until the blue air
is clean
and the green lawn drifts with
mauled feathers
and the broad cropped yard
blossoms
in tiny glass-eyed heads turned
toward death
and nothing, nothing sings.

Tiresias

It was August—you knew
by the dry wind and the sun
thumping your back and shoulders
hot till the hairs frizzed.
I was alone—I'd walked off—
and the afternoon was hollow
so you could hear the trains
five far-off miles over the lake,
the lake air shrill with whistles
and loons, old knobbly twigs
set off like sulfur matches
where a man stepped, and leaves
waiting high up to catch the fire.

I was confused. I fell a lot
so as to feel stiff flower stems
on the heels of my hands,
and I could hear the others
laughing along the beach.
I fell plenty, so the woodlots
wrote summer on my palms,
and this one time I went down
I put my hand out—half to break
falling, half to help getting up—
and here was the old tree.

Everyone's touched trees.
You know them either smooth
like the skin of a birch
with just enough scoring
to let you know you've got
a piece of wood men didn't work
or like maple and oak

ragged enough to bring blood.
This was neither—or both.
This one was dead, the bark of it
was peeled to the bare trunk.
I could feel the weathering,
the wide cracks opened up,
life long gone out of it.

I drew my fingers up the rough
of the tree—that shell eaten out,
or lightning-struck, or killed by age—
until I caught its lowest limb.
I wanted to pull higher, wanted
to climb, wanted the top of it
now I'd felt the direction it took.
What's queer is I couldn't know
it had a top. It might have split
above my hands, and its snarled
branches be fifty feet away
elbowed under a berry scrub.

Damn blindness! Crotchety
and kinless, I've damned it
for slaving me to duller senses—
as the stench of rain on the earth
hurts my head, and heavy storms
ache on my eardrums long before
I hear thunder. I'm a history
of weathers, and the diary
the foolish seasons fumble at:
My ribs crack around spring
and cave in on autumn. My tongue
is cattail and icicle, my hands

flower and frost. Soft insects
and milkweed brush my bare chest,
but drift off before I catch them.

Witness: Holding the sun
sticky between my shoulder blades
I hear loons, trains, laughter,
smell petals pinched under me,
cool my cheek against this old wood.
It was a good-sized tree, and I
can guess how deep a shade it cast
on summer, years before falling—
but guessing's not enough.

The others, when this season ends,
wear visions from the normal world
colored and clear; they know
dimensions, know five ways
the measure of material things,
blunder into nothing. You learn
from seventy smothered years
the differences in men, and how
senses peeled to their rawest
grope short of truth, always, until
you no more dare ask after it.

Shadows

1.

Field creatures
before they die
glimpse the owl's
moony outline.

Like the dream
of a cloak,
a knife asleep
in its folds,

like wisdom
in its own shade
despising
the bodily,

one dropped wing
harrows them
and the dust
under.

2.

Goslings, stupid
in barnyards,
know the shape
of the hawk.

Their brains have
a nervous itch
for whatever
rides the air—

for a dark kite
broken away
from its string;
for joined leaves;

for any cloud
presuming
to grow wings
and be death.

3.

Shadows. Night
makes its own,
day contrives them
out of light.

They are blood
or nothing;
they are
a natural mask

of foresights,
of small breath
made visible
to be stricken.

In the fields
they glide
and are silent
to coax silence.

"the BIRD
pursues the BEE
and KISSES it"

is a painting by
Miró. It tells how
the bee in aimless
flight has settled
upon the indolence
of one flower, how
the enchanted bird
encounters a sweet
tracing in the air
and follows it down
to the bee swaying
on his tall blossom.
The comfortable bee
tingles from pollen;
the enchanted bird
is giddy with light.
In Miró's painting
they meet only when
the garden turns
its deepest corner.
Nothing has led here
but honeyed words.

Lines for Suzanne

Possibly you are dead
on a hill in Seattle,
and the western rain
has made one small grotto
of your skull where
the boat of my thoughts
turns in the deep dark.

If you are already dead
I imagine you unmarked,
your delicate soft bones
pale and blue as rain;
if you are dead, no one,
not even an enemy,
would crush you with stone.

And if you are not dead
then surely you are dying.
Once you told me: It looks
as if I might make thirty,
I hadn't planned on that,
I'll have to invent
my whole life over again.

When you are truly dead
we shall make a parade,
we friends surviving you:
walk and smoke together,
cupping our sad words
so not to wipe quite away
the wet of your kisses.

A Fear of Crowds

In the spring resurrection
kites carried her to God
and hung her from a cloud
blue as paper and smoke,

her figure boyish, skewed,
her wrists and ankles bruised.
Children with their fathers
tripped in the soft fields,

the air pounded with kites.
Strings from heaven to earth
tangled in her braided hair.
She was a vehicle blown mad.

Now the summer is here
and the wind's decalogues
have died to a solo voice;
we are on a beach, lying

on our sugary elbows.
The sun cannot be looked at,
but we believe her saviour
sailed riderless out of sight.

The Man with the Blind Wife

has no one keeping an eye
on him, can do nothing
with gesture or the look
on his face, must contrive

that all his man's arts
flower in words, cadence,
and his walk be a poem;
caring for her, he knows

how one misstep clouds
her daydreaming, and how
he may never be happy
or some other way cruel.

Lines for Later Anniversaries

Husbands each one of us, we've wed
reality. God, nothing's new-
hid in the pangs of puberty;
them we realized, they share our beds,

we've no room else. Innocent girls
whose quaint hemlines below the knees
inveigled us to learn their thighs;
metal-green corridors of girls

slamming toward us with breasts a-dance;
cloakrooms, schoolyards of girls we loved
to think of loving up, and hugged
nights-long in slept Edens of chance

against the unhealed parts of us—
naked and white as bone their shades
blur the ripe aisles where once we fed
our minds their fleshy sustenance.

All present girls are myths revived;
dreamt ribs. Like bachelors we itch,
fall out of sleep, but dare not touch
where waking visions turn out wives.

I Wish in the City of Your Heart

I wish in the city of your heart
you would let me be the street
where you walk when you are most
yourself. I imagine the houses:
It has been raining, but the rain
is done and the children kept home
have begun opening their doors.

Two Men

When the poet makes love to her, she thinks
of the mechanic. When the poet is loving
her, she thinks, if she thinks of anyone,
of the mechanic. When the poet makes love
to her with his soft hands, she thinks, if
she thinks of anything, about her mechanic,
his hard hands callused and rough-cornered.
When the poet makes love to her she thinks
not how gentle are his hands on her skin,
but how awfully coarse are mechanic hands,
how they bruise her, how she prefers them.
When the poet makes love to her and she is
thinking of the mechanic, the old memories
sustain her patience with the poet's hands
which are so gentle she can scarcely feel
him caressing her secret places. How long
it takes him to bring her up to pleasure!
What she remembers is: how the mechanic has
hurt her, how she knew she was being loved.
When the poet makes love to her this last
time, she does not need to apologize to him
for saying goodbye, does not feel any guilt,
does not have to do anything at all except
lift the telephone to ring up the mechanic
and lie in the empty bed knowing that even
if her skin will never again make the sound
of silk under a poet's touch, she is beloved
of a man who tends all day to cold machines,
who knows a difference between work and love.

When We Are Old

Young women when we are old
hurry us too fast toward truth;
they mean us no harm, they mean
to wish us only the best
of the cold years remaining.

One, leaning on a pillow,
whispers: I will help you, I
will teach you. In return,
love me with all your wisdom.
She kisses our eyes. We die.

How much wisdom can a man
give up? Now we are gone gray
it was a single knowledge
rattled around in our heads;
to tell it was the murder.

The one we tried most to love
whispered: Touch me, with a word
touch me to the heart. We did.
We let out the last secret.
In the darkened room, she smiled.

When we wake alone the day
is bleak, icebound. This time
it is neighbors whispering,
black cars waiting to drive us
one last time to bed.

Byzantium Again

I hold nothing against this country. Nothing.
Every forty-five minutes the buses depart
Stinking, blue-smoking, certain every start
They make leads them to somewhere, means something.

I board none of them; I am not made hungry
By the cinematic vision of half the seats empty,
Frame after frame flickering past my slow eye
And the theme of tire treads piling to the sky.

None of the motions rouse me, nor the sounds
Prologue to motion, nor the wish brought to ground
At the rims of the terminals. Listen hard:
Metal grates metal; you cannot purse one word

Out of the noises, for they are not truly of coins
But only of tokens punched out of light boxes;
They drop in the trampled street, the old men turn,
The single-minded young hitch their Rolleiflexes.

But who can say if the land the buses reach
Is not alread splendidly pulled down?
Every forty-five minutes the buses return
Bearing not silver, but tarnish from the beaches.

The stink is the same, the blue smoke as vile,
The pictures as before in their black frames blank;
The hound with the blinded eye scents how the miles
Lead by craft to no prey, and no master's thanks.

Old emperors bestrode blue-eared elephants
And boy drivers wore silk turbans in whose shade
Were fixed the grins of men wed to wonderlands.
The world we dream is a journey not to be made.

The Marijuana Smokers

1. The Boredom that Comes of Loneliness

In this street night after night
the wheels murmur across concrete,
tires in the hot sunset cry out
at the end of the block, the children
called in for bed draw over the curbs
the oilless wagons and doll carriages;
an orange ball lies in the gutter
day after day, never in the same place
one sun to the next; downhill winds
roll and roll, dust, leaves, papers
the children peel from soft candies.

The sun, the wind, they have no place
to go; the children have no place to go
though they have destinies; the wheels
turn and turn, seeming to participate
in arrivals and departures; the sun
returns in the mornings, and the wind,
to the same dust, the same dry leaves,
the voices and toys of remembered lives
handing on their names a hundred years.

We say to ourselves: *I am going away,*
for just a little while, a half-hour,
a weekend, only a lifetime or less—
to buy some cigarettes, get some air,
mail a letter, meet a friend for coffee,
pace in the sun and make shadows. We say:
I'm coming right back. Wait up for me.

Here comes the sun across the street
and in through the picture window;
it sits on the edges of the furniture
and plays the black keys of the piano;

it rises stiffly from the hard bench,
moves over the carpet, leaves ashes
glowing in the green ashtray; it crawls
up over the sill and drops to the lawn.
Look, how it muddles in the junipers.
Later we hear it rolling on the roof,
up to the ridgepole and over and off;
there it goes, out through the poplars,
the wind rippling behind it, noisy,
like the whisper of axles going dry.

Before midnight the neighbors come home.
The sound of the tread of their tires
is sticky, like the gold candy papers,
catching up gravel from the driveways;
through our windows open and screened
the voices of the neighbors are metal
extrusions out of darkness, half-private,
cut off all at once behind back doors.

If at this hour we take on the risk
of going to sleep, what will we miss?
The moon, at any given moment, pretends
balance on the wires beyond the poplars.

2. *The Persistence of First Love*

You walked with your young man
as ritual has it—not
hand-holding, not arm-in-arm,
but the way friends go along
streets; the way wet bike tires
track the pavements, each tread
discrete some little distance,
bending back to touch and cross
its twin, a design like braid

unwound. So you two touched
a casual shoulder, the back
of a bare hand April-warm.

You paused just at the place
where the path to your porch
met the sidewalk, and you said:
Oh, Michael, thinking how calm
he was, how many Aprils
he had shepherded you home
in the years' first sweet rains,
how much you sensed—by him—
your growing up and the depths
your young desires went down to,
as if to sow excitements
under the dormant earth.

Oh, Michael, I was looking
down at this broken path,
this old cement. I thought:
Now every single time
I see cracks in a sidewalk
they will remind me of you—
Nature reaching through for me.
To which—as you have told it—
Michael said nothing at all,
but kissed you on the forehead,
waved goodbye from the corner,
and left to become a priest.

So now the whole paved world
buckles under you, grass
squeezes up at your feet
and black earth is a craze
to every horizon.
God help the two of us.

What can I be for you
except some solemn spider
at the center of his web—
ready to encumber you,
to punish you with Michael
and your angelic childhood?

3. *The Weekend Away*

We are hardly civilized.
How long it has been
since we were fully clothed,
since the bed was made,
since the cottage did not reek
from stale linens
and smoke and the odors
of pointless copulation,
do you remember?—
O delicious holiday!

Only, my god, how long
shall we go on so?
As in Olyesha's fictions,
all Natural order
stifles in our visions:
mornings, the coffeepot
in your blue hands
becomes a flower-sifter,
the kitchen floor
is littered with petals

and seeds which root
inside the black seams
of the linoleum—
by noon the curious plants
stand waist-high,

like lunatics we flay
them to the ground
and thresh their thin stems
against the walls;
the porous plaster crazes.

Just as the sun sets
we finish milling the grain,
the chaff is flushed
down the toilet, you fill
with perfume and salt
and sewing-basket eggs
the porcelain bowl
(your hands utensils!
a beater, a spatula)
stirring stirring stirring.

Into the oven go
the swollen green loaves
and out come: what?
Rainbows, each slice a color.
We stuff ourselves,
wash it all down with beer;
by midnight we are bloated
as clouds, wildly hugging
each other in bed,
our faces wet with laughing.

4. Sunday Night

Tonight seems (our windows open,
the sky deadly black)
all that's left of the universe.

Stars are gone under
and the froth of the clouds like scum
drains them away;

we can feel the room beginning
to swing keel-over,
we can hear the wind rising on

its voyage. Windows
are smashed all around, people chuck
their belongings out:

books, long underwear, mistresses
pink in their nightgowns,
the landlord's cat and her kittens.

What are we doing,
lying fouled in each other's arms
while the world founders?

We can hear the chandeliers chink,
see the lamps spilling
kerosene on oilcloth tables,

choke on yellow smoke
hissing from the great ark of time —
fire and water,

the enterprise of destruction
(we once prayed for it)
nearly completed in one night.

We should crawl outside
to watch the panic, with such help
as we might offer

held back until the cave of Hell
looms — then scream out: *We
can save you! We can see you through!*

to those survivors
who do not deserve damnation
or have not lived there.

5. *The Smokers*

The fact is: we are
a painting in a blue frame
on some calcimined wall
inside a stucco house
where old men and women
outlive their dull lives.
The colors of the oils
have turned untrue; age
and the odd chemistries
of pigment and season
confound the eye—as if
the scene comprising us
lay decades deep, buried
under distance and dust.
Our flesh is not flesh,
but something of shaded
gold, honey of smoke
like an accretion found
on glass or chinaware
no one thinks to wash.

Even the furnishings
recede into a darkness:
the spare, brown sofa
with its legs brass-capped;
the cheap lamp which,
lighted, casts upward
round rainbow bubbles
(like the muted croak
of an underworld frog);
the picture framed inside
this frame, a dark Degas
upon whose raked stage

67

pink dancers rehearse
in an aura of withered
petals; the raw carpet
once orange. All these
under layers of filth
glow as if an eternal
source projected them
from the center of time.

And you. And I. How
untrue our two images
smoulder in the gloom.
Like a host and hostess
on the bottom of a pool
at an adult party,
here we perform—clothed,
decent and drunk, seen
through green shallows
doing whatever we do.
Here what we breathe
is more dense than air.
We are things with skins
so tight our very nerves
are squeezed to the bone,
if we lie still we feel
the marrow making blood
and the hum resonant
on every sense, our lungs
are liquid and violent.

The fact is: we are
a pale green aquarium
in a waterfront bar,
and we slide like eels
into the bubbling deep,
seeming stuck together

with our common mouth
impossible of breath;
seeming, as we touch down
to the graveled bottom
and wind in gray spirals
upward, like the caduceus
on a clinician's wall.
The drinkers, black men
with solemn yellow eyes,
watch us through the glass.
We amuse them, we touch,
we braid our two selves,
we look—though legless—
nothing if not obscene.

Pale fish, whose scale and fin
light enters and informs,
we swim the closed hours
(watch the drinkers fade
through windows into fog
and the neon flicker out),
swim all alone all night
(poor swishers enervated
and colorless as jelly),
fall, bump, and push off.
Savage, you turn on me,
fix on me your notched mouth,
swallow me. Dear predator,
one swimmer and another
make you a meal, dinner
invisible, such victims
as water gods devour.
I die. I am ballet
under a brackish sea,
sailless and unruddered.

I wheel and turn under,
belly up, stark white,
no blood in this skeleton
the bubbles nudge, nothing
but panic like mermaid hair
snarled in a mermaid comb.
And you: circling, nibbling
as if it gave you pleasure. . . .
To complain and not drown!
The fact is: we are
murderous. At noon
when the bar opens up
one drinker carrying
an amber glass to his mouth
will spy me floating, so—
gap-gilled, all but dead,
surfaced and adrift—
will pick me out, while you
doze out of sight in castles
tall on pebbles tinted gold.

A *Tapestry, a Poem*

Here unfolds the tale of the talents,
the grapes, the seven shrewd virgins,
Betsy Ross and the centaurs, the youth
with the certain wolf, Sergeant York,
and (not least) the THREE BLACK STONES.

I've little more to say about this:
It came to me as in a vision, as from
the town nearest Porlock. Nightingales
had been uncorked into my dim garden;
the Muse sat by, seeing to my shuttle.

I'd thought about doing the Unicorn—
and I'd thought about doing St. George,
too, earlier. I'd even thought about
La dame sans merci on La Grande Jatte,
except for that damned petit point.

Now it is done, I am immensely proud.
Sometimes we use it as a table cloth,
eat off it carefully. The few times
the children spill, I bite my tongue.
Look: It tells all there is about us.

Yankee Poet

A cup is bound to spill, a saucer to break,
Some blunder to bring on a clumsy lull
In civilized talk. I know. We're that full
Of Nature; a fair number of mistakes

Occur to us by instinct. But we are
Worth all the crockery. We make a show
For the sophisticated folks; we do
A homely trick or two with stones and stars;

We own, ruefully, to some trafficking
With Satan, and a middling taste for hate
Into the bargain. Virtue and sin debate
At the town meetings of our souls. I think

New England makes more poems because it lies
So far from Heaven and so near to Hell.
We know them both, and the old glaciers tell
Us truths in granite. Yet we are not wise.

Only this morning I raked up some leaves
The frost knocked down, but what they might have meant—
Those portents of mortality, gravely sent—
I missed to praise the colors autumn gives.

I know. . . . It's foolish for a man to read
The splendid side of death. I ought instead
To say how grim it is to curl up dead
Across a green and gold October bed—

That's one way. Still, I hope my ignorance
Turns out to be real wisdom at the last.
You can't learn anything but from the past;
Tradition sets the straightest line to sense.

Say Girls in Shoe Ads:
"I go for a man who's tall!"

Me, for example,
a skinny kid
skyrocketed to skinny manhood—
my mother as a girl nicknamed
"Spindleshanks,"
my father off at Exeter
called "Master Bones"—

Me, the shy get of their clacking
sharp-hipped love,
who scowled school corridors
in trousers cuffless
and too tight at the crotch,
who ducked for awnings,
cracked his skull through exits,
stuck like two warped planks
out of bunk beds and camp cots—

Me, wickedly inside my slats,
taught in the nick of time
this lanky aphrodisia of height,
this lusty vertigo—
crying to the runt world:
Jump! ladies soft and small.
Shinny up for kisses.
Hang on for love.

Envoi

Sun in the mouth of the day,
Moon in the teeth of night—
Taste everything, they say;
Swallow nothing but light.

About the Author

Robley Wilson was born in Brunswick, Maine, in 1930. He received a Bachelor of Arts from Bowdoin College, a Master of Fine Arts from the University of Iowa, and in 1987 was granted a Doctor of Letters degree from Bowdoin. In 1983-84 he held a Guggenheim Fellowship in fiction. Wilson is the only writer to have won both of the major literary prizes offered by the University of Pittsburgh Press. He was the winner of the 1982 Drue Heinz Literature Prize for his third story collection, *Dancing for Men*, and the 1986 Agnes Lynch Starrett Poetry Prize for his first poetry collection, *Kingdoms of the Ordinary*. He is Professor of English at the University of Northern Iowa, and editor of *The North American Review*.

PITT POETRY SERIES

Ed Ochester, General Editor